MW00772134

LITTLE BOOK OF

LOEWE

Published in 2024 by Welbeck
An Imprint of HEADLINE PUBLISHING GROUP LIMITED

1

Cataloguing in Publication Data is available from the British Library

ISBN 9781035419647

Printed in China

Headline's policy is to use papers that are natural, renewable and recyclable products and made from wood grown in well-managed forests and other controlled sources. The logging and manufacturing processes are expected to conform to the environmental regulations of the country of origin.

HEADLINE PUBLISHING GROUP LIMITED
An Hachette UK Company
Carmelite House
50 Victoria Embankment
London EC4Y 0DZ

The authorised representative in the EEA is Hachette Ireland, 8 Castlecourt Centre, Castleknock Road, Castleknock, Dublin 15, D15 YF6A, Ireland

www.headline.co.uk
www.hachette.co.uk

LITTLE BOOK OF

LOEWE

The story of the iconic design house

JESSICA BUMPUS

WELBECK

CONTENTS

INTRODUCTION

With its viral fashion moments fuelled by forward-thinking design, alongside a heritage steeped in leather craft, and a creative director who knows how to push style boundaries, the Spanish fashion house Loewe has become one of the most popular luxury fashion brands in recent times. Arguably, it is the brand of the moment.

*V*ogue editor Anna Wintour, Ariana Grande, Jamie Dornan, Emilia Clarke, Alexa Chung, Dua Lipa, Karlie Kloss, Timothée Chalamet and Callum Turner are among those who wear the brand's distinct blend of cool, intelligent and a little bit quirky, and can be spotted front row.

It is a favourite on the red carpet, among influencers and fashion insiders, and is one of the most anticipated shows of Paris Fashion Week each season, where the trends are set and defined.

You won't find Loewe falling in line with any other fashion house, or confirming the season's penchant for a certain colour or shape. Part of the brand's current – and renewed – appeal is that it thinks outside the box; takes ideas and inspirations that

OPPOSITE The model Emily Ratajkowski is a guest at the Loewe Womenswear autumn/winter 2024–25 show, Paris Fashion Week, 2024.

LEFT The current Loewe creative director Jonathan Anderson at the brand's autumn/ winter 2015–16 show in Paris, 2015.

shouldn't work, or you think couldn't work (examples include balloon shoes, grass trousers and unfastened bras dangling from dresses) and suddenly they do. It is avant-garde design at its best, managing to combine both cult status and commercial viability.

This is all down to its current creative director, Jonathan Anderson, who was appointed to the role in 2013. Having already earned himself a reputation for being a wunderkind designer in London – he started out in menswear but, such was the popularity of his designs, he branched out into womenswear

– it was obvious he was destined for a big fashion house. Though Loewe might not have been, at the time, the most obvious choice.

However, since then, Anderson has turned the output of the heritage leather house – which had struggled to catch the fashion limelight in previous years – into a raging *tour de force* and one that extends beyond fashion. Art and design affiliations are key to the brand's modern DNA, enabling it to expand beyond the reach of the catwalk.

In the second quarter of 2023, Loewe was namechecked as being the most in-demand brand globally by The Lyst Index. The Loewe Anagram tank top and the raffia tote were two of the list's hottest items (and they are street-style favourites). But these are just the latest in a long line of "It" items. There is the Puzzle

BELOW The Loewe Anagram tank top, a simple but effective – and in-demand – piece.

LEFT Kaia Gerber
modelling Loewe
autumn/winter
2020–21, Paris
Fashion Week, 2020.

bag, arguably the brand's biggest "It" bag since the Amazona back in the 1970s; perfume and candles have been introduced; there is jewellery (a Loewe × Lynda Benglis jewellery collaboration in May 2024 saw pieces knotted, poured and pleated) and striking eyewear. Small leather accessories have harnessed the history of the house to fun and characterful effect for a collection of cute coin purse animals, key chains and customizable bits.

OPPOSITE A memorable Loewe look as modelled by Mona Tougaard for autumn/winter 2019, Paris Fashion Week, 2019.

RIGHT Shimmer and sequins at a shine-filled Loewe spring/summer 2022 show, Paris Fashion Week, 2021.

It is a brand known for its artsy designs with an intellectual edge, and has become a go-to name for brilliant, and sometimes bonkers, designs – which resonates with a whole new generation.

In 2023, Anderson for Loewe (and his own label) won the biggest prize at the Fashion Awards in London, deemed the Oscars of the fashion industry, scooping Designer of the Year (having previously won awards for his own brand JW Anderson).

This came off the back of further successes that year – Maggie Smith became a campaign star for the brand, which got everyone talking. Anderson has pioneered the use of unexpected faces in his campaigns and collaborations in recent years, and his front row is always full of the very newest and about-to-be-well-known names (recently *Masters of the Air*'s Anthony Boyle, *Slow Horses*' Jack Lowden and *Bridgerton*'s Luke Newton were all spotted at the spring/summer 2025 menswear show). Meanwhile, hit runway collections included those that turned clothes seemingly into ghostly entities and another that explored mosaic techniques inspired by Byzantine art.

Loewe started 2024 well, too. Andrea Riseborough in black and red plaid; Jodie Foster in custom navy blue; and Greta Lee in a monochrome halter gown at the Oscars. Zendaya has dazzled in custom looks for her *Challengers* tour, and Anderson himself created the costumes for the film. Pertinently, the house sponsored the 2024 Met Gala. A recent Instagram story showed Jonathan Anderson and a bus full of the brand's smiling ambassadors and friends, including Dan Levy, Alison Oliver, Ambika Mod and Ayo Edebiri, en route to the star-studded night. Loewe had also dressed the event's formidable co-host, Anna Wintour, in a long coat inspired by tailoring from the autumn/winter 2024 collection. One wonders how Anderson fits it all in, especially running his eponymous brand, too (he has separate phones for both jobs, which probably helps...)

OPPOSITE *Vogue* editor Anna Wintour was dressed by the brand at the 2024 Met Gala in a custom floral coat.

LEFT The actress
Andrea Riseborough
wore autumn/
winter 2024 Loewe
at the 96th Annual
Academy Awards
on 10 March 2024
in Hollywood.

Loewe's glowing reputation is quite a different story from 20 years ago when the brand, it seemed, was still in the stages of reawakening – and to varying degrees of success as different designers tried their hand at the helm. To look back at some of those collections now, it would be difficult to recognize the house as it is today. It feels more alive, modern and in touch under Anderson, but the world of fashion has also changed.

Where other fashion houses have an overarching legacy or unwavering style and aesthetic, in many ways the house of Loewe has always been segmented. Because of this, it can be identified through its different eras, as this book will explore. There is a history and then a renaissance, a time of experimentation as well as a surprise appointment that has changed the course of the house's future – and its success.

There is one thing that remains unchanged in the brand's legacy since it began: the question of how exactly one pronounces the name Loewe. Notably, it is not "low", as is often thought. The "w" leads into a "v" so it is actually "lo weh ve", or "low-ay-vay".

But don't worry too much about getting it wrong. The brand is not one to take itself too seriously on this front, and happily plays on this confusion. In 2018, it asked the models who walked the show that season to pronounce it – they all said it differently; and more recently the "word" became the subject of the brand's latest campaign, featuring Aubrey Plaza and Dan Levy as though at a spelling bee. Throughout the short film, Plaza's different characters fail to spell the word correctly. The brand's name is in fact the name of Enrique Loewe, a German craftsman who joined a collective of Spanish leather artisans. The house is named after him, and his story begins in nineteenth-century Madrid.

OPPOSITE Timothée
Chalamet at the
Loewe menswear
autumn/winter
2023–24 show, Paris
Fashion Week, 2023.

RIGHT Friend of the
brand Dan Levy wore
Loewe at the 2024
Met Gala.

LEFT The famous
Loewe (pronounced
"lo weh ve")
company logo and
anagram motif.

LEFT Florals at the Loewe autumn/winter 2024 show, Paris Fashion Week, 2024.

OPPOSITE Alexa Chung in 2023 at *British Vogue*'s Forces For Change at The MAINE Mayfair, London, wearing Loewe autumn/winter 2023.

IN THE
BEGINNING

THE LEGACY OF LOEWE

Enrique Loewe left more than a lasting legacy about how to pronounce his name. The history of Loewe starts in 1846 when a collection of Spanish artisans opened a leather workshop on a street named calle Lobo in Madrid. As the brand tells it, the atelier initially made small leather goods, like purses, wallets, cigarette and jewellery cases, as well as frames.

E nrique Loewe Roessberg came to settle in Madrid, where he was impressed by the artisans' knowledge and the quality of their materials; he joined the workshop in 1872, bringing prodigious technical skills with him, which complemented the artisans' craftsmanship and creativity. And so began Loewe.

Originally called E. Loewe, around 1892 a large store and workshop on calle Principe opened. It was described as a leather goods factory – it produced small leather goods and began to design women's handbags.

By 1905, Loewe had become an official supplier to the Spanish Royal Crown, and by 1910 began its expansion across Spain: it opened two stores in Barcelona, and a flagship in central

OPPOSITE The Loewe store on Gran Vía, Madrid.

Madrid's Gran Vía opened in 1939. The architect Francisco Ferrer Bartolomé later added curved windows to the latter, which meant that the view of the interiors was not visible to passers-by but products could be highlighted against large curtains. It was considered a new concept that helped to build the brand's luxury image.

Window displays have long been a part of its heritage. Today, notably, Loewe is well known for its striking window displays, which can seem more like art installations, and its impactful visuals. In an interesting twist of serendipity, Jonathan Anderson's own career began as a visual merchandiser for Prada. Between 1945 and 1978, José Pérez de Rozas was in charge of creating the Loewe window displays, which were known for being theatrical and creative, artworks to be revealed with great anticipation each season (the correlation continues).

The 1950s saw the brand open a leather factory in the centre of Madrid as well as a school of leather craft in which a structure of teachers and apprentices made sure knowledge would be passed down through the generations. The brand began to amass a glamorous clientele – even royalty. Princess Grace of Monaco numbered among their patrons. Supposedly, there is a carefully preserved book of signatures at the Gran Vía Loewe store that displays these glamorous customers.

The following decade saw a spate of store openings, from calle Serrano in Madrid, deemed a very prestigious area, to San Sebastián, Valencia, Tenerife and Tangier. By then it was the third generation Enrique Loewe Knappe who led the house. He enlisted the architect Javier Carvajal to design the space in Madrid, which had an avant-garde feel.

It was in 1963 that Loewe came to London. Today, Loewe's flagship store in the capital can be found on New Bond Street at numbers 41–42, a three-storey heritage property, Casa Loewe.

OPPOSITE At a Loewe fashion show in New York at the Plaza Hotel in 1983.

With interiors designed by the brand's creative director Jonathan Anderson, it features a commanding spiral staircase at its centre, as well as a pop-up space for capsule collections and art collections.

Besides its affinity for art and craft, Loewe is recognizable for its "Anagram" motif logo, which was designed by Vicente Vela in 1970. Its inspiration comes from branding irons used to mark high quality leather, and the logo features four Ls, ornate in design, which are repeated to make a square formation. It feels historical, refined and also slightly whimsical, which is arguably a little bit of what the brand is about today under the creative direction of Anderson.

The 1960s and 1970s was a time of international expansion for the brand with women's ready-to-wear collections debuting in 1960 and store openings across Asia with Tokyo, in 1973, among them. According to *Vogue.com*, during this time the late Karl Lagerfeld and Giorgio Armani did early stints designing at Loewe.

A women's fragrance was launched in 1972 – L de Loewe – and then Loewe Pour Homme debuted in 1974. These were followed by Aire in 1985, Esencia in 1987, Aura in 1994, Agua in 2000, Solo in 2004, 7 in 2010, 001 in 2016 and Earth in 2022, among others. A menswear collection launched in 1983.

In 1985, a significant thing happened for the brand, its website notes: Louis Vuitton, which would later become the LVMH luxury conglomerate, became a shareholder in Loewe. (Over the course of the following years, the group – formed in 1987 – bought various fashion houses such as Celine, Kenzo and Marc Jacobs, making it the luxury power stable it is today.) At this time, Loewe was, according to the brand, experiencing an increased presence in Asia with stores in Japan, Singapore and China. In 1996, the now-formed LVMH group acquired Loewe and began to work on revitalizing its womenswear. And tasked with taking on the job was the Cuban-American fashion designer Narciso Rodriguez, appointed in 1997.

It was a time when there was a lot of movement going on in the fashion industry, and many new and exciting names were also emerging. John Galliano had just been at Givenchy, a job Alexander McQueen took with Galliano's move to Dior. *WWD* reported that the hire of Rodriguez was similar to that of Marc Jacobs at Louis Vuitton – taking a buzzy new name and putting it at a heritage house to transform it, in a bid to compete with the likes of Gucci and Hermès. Rodriguez's first official presentation was slated for the autumn/winter 1998 season. The designer had come from brands including Cerruti, TSE and Calvin Klein, but perhaps more notably he designed the wedding dress for 1990s style icon, and his close friend, Carolyn Bessette-Kennedy. Rodriguez's design for her, a bias-cut gown, propelled him to international fame, and is still much referenced to this day for its pared-back, minimalist style.

The designer was also known for his precise tailoring and clean aesthetic, which at the time he told *WWD* he thought would work well with Loewe's focus on quality. He said that he wanted to bring a sexier feel to collections. Rodriguez's first offering played to the strength of his sleek style and chimed with the way fashion was going at the turn of the millennium: minimalist, clean and modern. He did separates in neutral block colours; a lace cut-out on the back of a black column dress revealed its wearer's behind as though butterfly wings misplaced, certainly a sexier take as he had promised.

Spring/summer 1999 put a focus on silver (a popular future-facing colour choice for fashion at the time), and grey/blue tones for more casual but clean separates. Autumn/winter 1999 became more sultry with sheath shifts, macs and boots and a palette of black and beige.

The first collection from the Spanish fashion house to have been posted on *Vogue.com* was spring/summer 2000 (back in the early 2000s, typically, designer collections would only be glimpsed in the supplements of fashion magazines or in newspaper reports, or the whole collection seen in a speciality title). The opening look was a white halter dress, and the anonymous reviewer/commentary went on to point out that it was the dominant colour of the collection with flourishes here and there of yellow, tan and blue. They also commented that Rodriguez had done a respectable job of nodding to the heritage of the brand.

While the spring/summer 2000 collection is both typically Narciso Rodriguez in feel and millennium in look, it is very different from the Loewe we know today. The autumn/winter 2000 collection received favourable reviews from *Vogue* and was applauded for its elegance and control; it featured a honey and tan colour palette and black shift dresses.

Spring/summer 2001 went in a similar vein to the previous two collections in terms of shapes; there were shirts and belts, it was still very minimalist, with shots of red, and it felt quite sexy.

OPPOSITE Fashion designer Narciso Rodriguez at the end of the spring/summer 2001 Loewe show, Paris Fashion Week, 2000.

OPPOSITE Tactile
Loewe for autumn/
winter 1999–2000.

RIGHT A minimalist
take at Loewe for
spring/summer
2001, Paris Fashion
Week, 2000.

But by the autumn/winter 2001 show, held in March 2001, Rodriguez took his final bow as Loewe's designer – reportedly to focus on his new signature line. His last collection was much of the same, strong shapes with some shimmer and shine. But perhaps just not quite enough shine.

José Enrique Ona Selfa designed his first collection for Loewe for the autumn/winter 2002 season, which *Vogue.com* noted as being a "decent attempt" in its review, which is a mix of praise and criticism. The collection was a rainbow of brown tones, from yellows to butterscotch and toffee, with cream and also black. Again, it was a lot about separates and was led by a workwear kind of mentality.

There then appears to be a gap in coverage. The catwalk photography agency *First View* has the autumn/winter 2002 show, and then leaps forward to spring/summer 2006. And by autumn/winter 2007, it seems the brand identity was still being called into question by reviewers. A recurring query would be: how does a brand steeped in a leather heritage do summer?

In 2008, Brit designer Stuart Vevers (formerly of Calvin Klein, Mulberry, Louis Vuitton and Bottega Veneta, and part of the new wave of London talent which included Giles Deacon and Katie Grand) was appointed as creative director at Loewe. It was a move that came with great anticipation. There was an immediate buzz about what Vevers could and would do. Having remade Mulberry as a contemporary and highly coveted label, he is credited as having fuelled the "It"-bag mania of the time. During his tenure at Loewe, there were a lot more accessories, naturally; he brought more personality to the collections and got good reviews. He created outfits and whole looks – which weren't always necessarily even dictated by the leather.

For autumn/winter 2009, the brand opted for a runway show. Previously, the house had held static presentations (just like

LEFT Loewe autumn winter 2009–10, by Stuart Vevers.

ABOVE Stuart Vevers, the then newly crowned creative director at Loewe at the brand's spring/summer 2009 collection, showcased at Les Folies Bergère during Paris Fashion Week, 2008.

he shows in presenting the season's new wares, but typically operating on a smaller scale) where the craftsmanship could be appreciated up close. It is a move that seems to have changed the dynamic and perception of the brand.

For spring/summer 2010 there were lots of crop tops, macs and dresses, and some great bags as one would expect from a bag maestro.

In the 2020s, there is a penchant in luxury fashion for turning the humble shopping bag into something high-end. This is something Vevers was already doing back in the 2010s, a note of the surreal, pertinently, that has become the calling card of the house under Anderson's watch.

For autumn/winter 2010, the Ava bag was introduced – inspired by the actress Ava Gardner, who had apparently signed a visitor book at Loewe's Madrid archive. The bag was a two-handled design, while the collection had a 1940s feel with stoles, skirt suits and tuxedos.

The spring/summer 2011 season was quite the opposite, opening with a pink dress and yellow bag. Silhouettes were belted, there were little shorts and fringing details, and bright colours galore.

A 1960s silhouette, secretary looks and sculpted dresses made for the autumn/winter 2011 collection; while spring/summer 2012 was prints and patterns, below-the-knee skirts and red, white and blue.

By the autumn/winter 2012 collection, Vevers had been at Loewe for four years. He showed bomber and varsity jackets, splaying skirts and fluffy dresses, and leather ponchos. It was both buttoned-up and 1960s, a bit Hitchcock.

PPOSITE Designer
iles Deacon, stylist
atie Grand and
newe creative
rector Stuart
evers at the UK
unch of Loewe on
ount Street (since
osed), 2011.

GHT Loewe's
utumn/winter 2010.

Elena Ivanovna Diakonova, or Gala Dalí, the artist Salvador's wife, inspired the spring/summer 2013 collection. It was handcrafted, youthful, pops of orange-red and very Spanish in feel. With pencil skirts and jackets, there was also a slick and luxe utility element with big pockets, belts and hoods.

Femmes fatales led the way for the autumn/winter 2013 season, which was a prevailing trend at the time. Big coats and boxy blouson shapes, it was more Hitchcock, this time with big hair. There were geometric graphics on leather tops and skirts. It felt stronger and more impactful than seasons before. It would, however, be Vevers's last collection for the house. He would next head off to Coach, where he also excelled.

In early 2013, something very interesting happened in the fashion world. PPR, now known as Kering, another luxury conglomerate, bought a 51 per cent stake in the young London fashion brand Christopher Kane. It was exciting news – and, one could note, echoed the moves of the 1990s when big houses were looking to young designers to make their fortune. Especially because, in September of that year, it was announced that LVMH was taking a minority stake in JW Anderson, the label of Jonathan Anderson, arguably the most exciting designer to have emerged in London since Christopher Kane.

Anderson's increasingly gender-neutral collections that had both a crafty folk and modern art feel were garnering great attention in fashion and his shows went from being among a one-day menswear schedule to the highlight of London Fashion Week womenswear.

But not only did LVMH acquire a minority stake in JW Anderson – they also appointed him as creative director of Loewe. An exciting new chapter for the fashion house was about to begin. Over a decade later, it is still thriving.

OPPOSITE Hitchcock vibes for autumn/winter 2013.

THE JONATHAN
ANDERSON YEARS

A NEW ERA

Born in Northern Ireland, Jonathan William Anderson
established his own label JW Anderson in 2008 at the
tender age of 24, and was immediately noted as someone
to be excited about. Disclaimer, I worked at *British Vogue*
on the website at this time and insisted we
interview him for this very reason.

Loewe's first output with Jonathan Anderson at the helm was for spring/summer 2015, and it was a menswear collection. The designer had produced a tome of images captured by the photographer Jamie Hawkesworth, and held a presentation at Loewe's Paris HQ. The fashion journalist Tim Blanks gave the designer high praise in his review, noting that there was quite a strong presence of him and his own label, JW Anderson, in the collection. Indeed, it was not archival, and the images captured for the tome show turned-up trousers and striped tops and ponchos. It felt young and nostalgic, fresh. Not pastiche or homage-y.

OPPOSITE At the menswear spring/summer 2015 preview.

An eagerly awaited womenswear collection came in September 2014. Held at the UNESCO building in Paris – where Anderson has often shown – looks were layered and felt organic, and showed early signs of the designer's self-confessed devotion to craft. Leather trousers boasted thick waists and came in bright colours, bows perched upon their hips, and teamed with T-shirts featuring idyllic scenes. Dresses were like torn strips pieced together to Flintstone effect. The fashion critic at *The New York Times*, Vanessa Friedman, said she felt it was a not a resolved collection and pointed out the volume of handbags that made an appearance on the runway.

In 2015, as would become the norm for the house, another menswear collection appeared for autumn/winter, expanding the brand's reach and its aesthetic appeal. The autumn/winter 2015 womenswear collection was very 1980s in shape and colour, a little retro, jarring in a cool kind of way. Skirts were below the knee and pleated, waists belted and jackets and coats on the statement side. Silver, red, green, blue, geometric patterns and more bags. It was a solid follow-up to his previous womenswear collection with key looks that spring to mind, even now.

Spring/summer 2016 went craftier and more tactile. What looked like shattered mosaic mirror shards smothered arms on dresses, or tunic bodices of others. Tinsel trailed the hem of a black skirt and geese appeared as a recurring motif. The collection that was heralded by the fashion critic Sarah Mower as an impressive one that would prompt LVMH to admire what Anderson was up to.

Along with the likes of Kim Jones – currently at Fendi and Dior – and Daniel Lee at Burberry, Anderson is among an exclusive cohort of British designers known globally, who have managed to propel British fashion minds to the forefront of the industry.

Anderson has said that his early fashion education was via magazines and the discount shop TK Maxx. He was the eldest of three children and, as told in an interview in *The Daily Telegraph*

OPPOSITE A standout look from the Loewe spring/summer 2015 show, Paris Fashion Week, 2014.

LEFT A 1980s feel
from Loewe autumn/
winter 2015–16, Paris
Fashion Week, 2015

RIGHT The simple appeal of a logo-ed Loewe T-shirt, a few years before the tank top made its presence known. Loewe spring/ summer 2016, Paris Fashion Week, 2015.

2024, says it is from his father that he gets his drive, while he gets his creative side from his mother, who was an English teacher. In the beginning, Anderson wanted to be an actor. He studied drama in Washington and auditioned for The Juilliard School in New York, but was rejected. He next went to work in a department store in Dublin and applied to Central Saint Martins, but was also rejected. He joined London College of Fashion on a menswear course but was soon diverted by an incredible opportunity. Manuela Pavesi, then fashion co-ordinator at Prada, offered him a job assisting her in dressing the windows of the London store. He has said that he learned a lot from her.

His own label first showed on schedule during London Fashion Week in 2008. Though he didn't pioneer unisex dressing, he did put a new spin on it, coupled with a focus on tactile craft. It was a modern interpretation of masculinity and femininity, which evolved to become an award-winning brand and earn legions of fans early on. Before long he presented a JW Anderson women's capsule collection in 2010.

For his own label he has won the British Fashion Award for Emerging Talent, Ready-to-Wear, in 2012; the New Establishment Award in 2013; and the Menswear Designer of the Year Award in 2014. In 2015, he won both Menswear and Womenswear Designer of the Year – it was the first time a brand had won the two. In 2017, he again won Womenswear Designer of the Year.

Sales were reportedly lagging at Loewe in 2013, when Vevers left. When Anderson took over there were rumours that he was tipped as successor to the creative directorship of another of LVMH's bigger brands – Louis Vuitton has often been namechecked among the gossip. When he took on the job, Anderson didn't rush to create a first collection, instead learning the company's history and trying to get to grips with everything – and telling his bosses to be patient, essentially. It was an astute move. The downfall of most designer debuts these days is pressure, anticipation and the inability for them to be able to grow and ease into the role. That was possible once upon a time – a pre-social media time. But today fashion is cut-throat: it is sink or swim, and among the industry trends that have emerged of late is designers being ousted after just one season, when they used to get three years if they were lucky.

Critics have often compared Anderson's own collections to Loewe's, as though they are a starter of some kind, or show one side of an evolving coin. No doubt, there are ideas and feelings that translate across them both, but the designer has always noted that when he's working on JW Anderson, he is working on JW Anderson; and when he's working on Loewe, he is working on Loewe.

In 2016, Loewe's cream mohair tweed asymmetric fringed dress with gold leaf Nappa leather bustier/corset was selected by *Vogue* fashion editor Kate Phelan as dress of the year for the Fashion Museum in Bath.

For autumn/winter 2016, Anderson's Loewe collection saw lots of accessories and cinched waists. It was a marriage of craft and leather, little trinkets to create a softer take on serious sculpted bodices and draped and layered looks. The designer experimented with tweed and there were cat-face necklaces and abundant gold jewellery elements – the final look was almost like a walking piece of jewellery, the model in a cascading take on chainmail.

The longer lengths he had been casting these past two seasons emerged once again for spring/summer 2017, a silhouette he generally stuck to for this collection. There were nods to the Spanish heritage of the house in all the different kinds of peasant blouses, which had balloon sleeves. Elsewhere, they were fringed. Heavy in accessories from shoes to bags, there was emphasis also on waists through pannier-type corset constructions.

OPPOSITE Lots of accessories for autumn/winter 2016

LEFT A crafty
patchwork feel
for Loewe spring/
summer 2017, Paris
Fashion Week, 2016.

OPPOSITE A cinched
waist and statement
silhouettes for
spring/summer 2017

Colours were bright and bold, orange, fuchsia and blue among them. This was kind of high octane, in contrast to the outgoing collections of Vevers.

Arguably autumn/winter 2017 went more romantic in feel. Off-the-shoulder dresses, frills that were more pretty than they were artsy, a sort of homespun luxury through the ages for a collection that was a brilliant collage of ideas, time periods and textures.

Among the accessories, which by now had become a strong talking point for the brand, were a bag in the shape of a cat and a Loewe-slogan tote, the brand logo on a slice of bread – surely the makings of a viral moment. The Puzzle bag came in orange with black spots, as well as plaid.

Spring/summer 2018 was described by the designer as being a little more bohemian and included pretty prairie dresses, some preppy polo styles, a pastel palette and jumpers and T-shirts that said "Loewe" across them, but were chopped up by fringe. There was patchwork in there, too.

For autumn/winter 2018, the show opened with a strapless bra fixed upon a T-shirt-like dress with fuzz at its hem. It was followed by dresses with twisted connectors of fabrics, lots of scarves or pussy bows trailing and cape coats.

Everything was textured for spring/summer 2019; the collection featured tactile colour in a craft-laden setting.

Autumn/winter 2019 came highly praised, full of historical notes and a distinct piece of headwear that *Elle* described as being part cloche and part animal, but overall magical.

Spring/summer 2020 went ethereal and a bit aristo: there was lots of lace, shapely panniers, ruffs and peplums, and there was a lingerie undertone to pieces which were both delicate and dramatic.

In contrast, autumn/winter 2020 was pared back. Pieces were more statement alone via gorgeous, elegant dresses and less accessory fuss.

A lookbook presented the spring/summer 2021 collection, which debuted during one of the coronavirus pandemic's lockdowns. Despite the state of the world, it was fun and vibrant and felt optimistic – even if, in the real world, no one really felt that way.

The model Freja Beha Erichsen starred in a series of images for autumn/winter 2021, for a collection that was pop-art regal and featured huge tassels, big decoration and heritage bags.

Back on the catwalk for spring/summer 2022, it was all about shape and structure, contorted versions of which were being explored. It is this collection that came with many viral moments.

Autumn/winter 2022 also played with composition and structure and dresses had cars implanted in their hems, the models now the drivers; there were dresses with luscious lips at the bust; and there was a general feeling of balloon mania throughout. Another hit.

Spring/summer 2023 was a mix of the horticultural and technological for dresses that were half blooms and ensembles that appeared like glitches, pixelated in their silhouette.

The latter idea filtered into autumn/winter 2023 for ghost-like garments of themselves. Shapes were simple but the motifs upon them were haunting – a former dress on a dress, the shadow of a trench. In complete contrast, the collection also featured Playmobil ensembles, giving the whole thing a sense of make-believe and otherworldliness of new dimensions.

Spring/summer 2024 saw incredible knitted poncho-cardigans and the addition of enlarged needle/pin decoration on tailoring and eveningwear. A dress worn by house friend Aubrey Plaza, which she wore to the Emmys, went viral – in yellow, it features an enlarged pin across the chest, prompting some Internet users to compare it to a Post-it. It is just one of many viral moments that had worked to make the house a hit again.

But Loewe is not just about the collections.

OPPOSITE Easy and literally breezy, cutouts at Loewe spring/summer 201

ARTS, CRAFTS AND CAMPAIGNS

LOEWE

Holidays 2022
Photographed by Lukas Wassmann

79 Greene Street, New
loewe

EXPANDING A LEGACY

On 14 May, Andrés Anza was announced as being the Loewe
Foundation Craft Prize winner 2024 for his ceramic totem, titled
"I only know what I have seen". It was described as being both
plant- and animal-like in form with its thousands of tiny spikes
across a sort of undulating surface that wound up to human height.
Not only was it life-sized, but it felt like it could be alive, as well.

Anza was the latest maker to scoop the prestigious prize,
at a ceremony held in Paris, where the actress Aubrey
Plaza – who had only recently starred in Loewe's witty
take on a spelling bee for its latest campaign – handed out the
accolade. A special mention went to three other creatives: Miki
Asai for a piece called "Still Life", Heechan Kim for a piece titled
"#16", and Emmanuel Boos for the coffee table "Comme un Lego".

In 2023, the prize went to Eriko Inazaki, whose work was
praised for its exceptional approach to decorative ceramics. Her
work featured tiny forms across the surface of the piece, which
looked organic as though something from the sea.

The prize, which takes place annually around spring, works to
highlight Loewe's beginnings as a collective craft workshop and

OPPOSITE Loewe has become well-known for its arresting campaigns.
Here in *WSJ. Magazine*, December 2022/January 2023 USA.

recognize the importance of craft and its culture today, while supporting the artists who explore its many forms. Loewe has long celebrated its own artisans, who it acknowledges as being master craftsmen (some of them have been with the brand for 50 years). They combine traditional techniques with evolving technologies to come up with new ideas and objects from the house's Madrid ateliers. There is also the Loewe School of Leather Craft in Madrid, which ensures that these skills are passed down through the generations. The prize, therefore, is entirely in keeping with Loewe's heritage and enables the brand to keep momentum beyond the world of leather – and beyond the seasons it, historically, was often deemed strongest, autumn and winter – while playing to its craftsmanship strength.

It was in 1988 that Loewe created the Loewe Foundation, originated by Enrique Loewe Lynch, a fourth-generation member of Loewe's founding family. Today it is led by his daughter, Sheila Loewe and, as president, she oversees the foundation's significant projects. These include the acclaimed international prizes for craft, as well as poetry; plus collaborations with leading arts festivals and supporting the world of dance.

Back in 1988, poetry was thought to be a neglected art form in Spain and so the Loewe Foundation set up an international prize to promote the best poetry in Spanish. According to the brand, it has become one of the most important prizes of its kind on the cultural calendar. In 2017, it celebrated three decades of support and a documentary to commemorate this was produced by the foundation and released on National Poetry Day.

A similar spotlight has been put on dance since 2007 when the foundation sponsored the dance season at Madrid's Teatro Real, an initiative that ran until 2018. In 2013, the foundation

became the official sponsor of Spain's Compañía Nacional de Danza, and also supported María Pagés's dance company with the aim to spread flamenco and Spanish culture around the world. The idea is to raise awareness of the dance world and support connections between dancers and audiences as well as specialists from other creative disciplines. Since 2011, the foundation has partnered with the Gran Teatre del Liceu, an opera house in Barcelona, and was the official sponsor of the Ballet de L'Opéra National de Lyon during its 2018–19 season.

But it was in 2016 that Jonathan Anderson, only three years after he arrived at the house, introduced the Loewe Foundation Craft Prize. There are 50,000 euros up for grabs for the winning

LEFT Tactile fringing
in a logo look for
spring/summer 201█

OPPOSITE Attentio█
to craft and
technique. Loewe
spring/summer 201█

LEFT From florals
to pixels, the Loewe
spring/summer 2023
collection had a lot
of ideas.

entry and the prize sets out to celebrate and support working artists who have vision and innovation for the future of craft.

In an interview with *AnOther Magazine* in 2017, Anderson spoke about how he felt people had an odd association when it came to craft and that it seemed to be nostalgic. He went on to point out that in a digital age, reconnecting with craft was a way to make one feel happy. A joy to be found among objects.

Artists and makers are invited to enter handmade works that show off exceptional craftsmanship as well as aesthetic value. It is judged by a panel of leading design experts, and results

BELOW Arty, striking sets have become a common feature of Loewe shows under the direction of Jonathan Anderson at Loewe. Here, spring/summer 202

in an exhibition and a catalogue to showcase the shortlisted pieces. The Loewe Foundation Craft Prize exhibition for 2024 ran until 9 June at the Palais de Tokyo, Paris, presenting the work of all 30 finalists. The whole aim of the foundation is to cover and support these types of fields of importance – such as craft, art, photography, poetry and dance. It sets out to provide support and education around these heritage pursuits and to promote their creativity. Anderson has said that "craft is the essence of Loewe", and pointed out that it is where modernity for the house lies. In 2002, the Loewe Foundation was awarded the Gold Medal for Merit in the Fine Arts, which is the highest honour to be granted by the Spanish government.

Loewe Crafted World took place in early 2024 and was the house's first public exhibition. An immersive experience, it went about exploring the Loewe history and its culture and dedication to crafts, charting 178 years of tradition as well as innovation – with rooms dedicated to the brand's inspirations – through six themed chapters. These ranged from *Born from the Hand* and *Welcome to Spain*, to *The Atelier*, *Fashion Without Limits* (which, aptly, is Anderson's collections), *United in Craft* and *Unexpected Dialogues*.

Loewe has the same commitment to art as it does to craft. Anderson often references artists/artwork in his collections, seeing art, design and craft as central to being human. Loewe commissioned 24 artists – including finalists and winners of the Loewe Foundation Craft Prize – to create an exhibition of lamps for Salone del Mobile 2024 in Milan which is the toast of the design world. For some, it was the first time they had worked with light. In 2022, then its sixth time there, it presented Weave, Restore, Renew at the showcase in which artisans created woven pieces with a new life.

Back in 2018, in a team-up between Loewe and the artist Anthea Hamilton, seven costumes were created for the annual Tate Britain commission, called The Squash. Contemporary artists are invited to create a new art installation in response to the grand spaces of the Duveen Galleries. Hamilton had made a stage for which a continuous performance of a single character would take place over six months – and they would be dressed in a "squash-like" costume. In collaboration with Anderson, Hamilton – who is known for her work that touches on art, design, fashion and popular culture – created seven costumes that referenced the shapes of squash or pumpkin as well as 1970s clothing. The idea was that performers would select a costume each day and that would impact how they were in the space.

OPPOSITE Big but elegant knits were among the most memorable looks for Loewe spring/ summer 2024.

OVERLEAF LEFT A Loewe advert circa the 2010s, before the arrival of Jonathan Anderson.

OVERLEAF RIGHT Impactful visuals have always been important to the Loewe brand, here spring/summer 201 by Steven Meisel.

Hôtel Ritz, Madrid,
Avril 2011

LOEWE
MADRID
1846

LOEWE

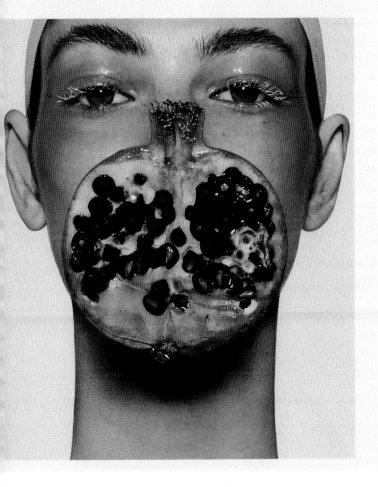

Collaborations have been key to Anderson's revamp of Loewe, keeping it contemporary, intriguing, challenging, fun and in keeping with the zeitgeist. Relationships run from the celebrities that feature in his campaigns, to collections and cultural events.

In 2023, Loewe collaborated with Studio Ghibli on a third and final collection of ready-to-wear, bags and accessories that depicted the wonderfully imaginative world of *Howl's Moving Castle*. The fire demon cropped up on the Puzzle bag – among others – and on a fluffy jumper for pieces that were charming and characterful, adding a whole new dimension to the brand, drawing in a broadened audience.

Besides the collections and collaborations, Loewe is well known now for its campaigns. During the pandemic, when shows went online and designers had to think about new ways to connect with the industry and their audience, Anderson came up with the clever idea to do a show-in-a-box. A day of livestreaming came with a special Loewe delivery: a dossier, or press pack, that detailed all the elements of his spring 2021 menswear collection. Arranged as an index file complete with dividers, it apparently weighed 10 pounds. Beginning with a word from Anderson, it then went on to explain inspiration, silhouette, a particular pattern for a look, plus profiles of the Loewe team, ending with the show invite (which of course was not really being held), all of which brilliantly tapped into an offline world anchored by crafty pursuits. As the brand described, it took the creative process and made it into a "sensorial experience", in which one could download the pattern from its website.

There have also been the seasonal campaigns, which have typically managed to make headlines owing to their intelligent casting.

POSITE The Loewe
ndow display on
enue Montaigne,
is.

Megan Rapinoe, football star, activist and advocate for the LGBTQIA+ community, featured in the autumn/winter 2020 campaign, photographed by Steven Meisel. In it, she bares her teeth and her image is featured next to a Loewe Hammock bag.

The Oscar-winner Anthony Hopkins starred in the autumn/winter 2022 campaign for the house, which was photographed by Juergen Teller. The singer Caroline Polachek joined him, as did the actress Jessie Buckley, singer HyunA, model Kaia Gerber, actor Josh O'Connor and sculptor Lynda Benglis, among others. Each was photographed in an unexpected setting and conveyed a strong sense of character in the images, which are playful.

Juergen Teller – a recurring collaborator – once again photographed the spring/summer 2023 campaign. The Loewe family continued to be built with Taylor Russell, Chloë Sevigny, Naomi Ackie and the director (of *Challengers*) Luca Guadagnino among its stars. The Oscar-winning costume designer Sandy Powell also featured.

For autumn/winter 2023, actors Takeshi Kitano, Aubrey Plaza, Murray Bartlett (of *The White Lotus* fame), Myha'la Herrold, Ruth Negga and Sonoya Mizuno joined musician Dev Hynes, model Xiao Wen Ju, artists Nairy Baghramian and Koo Jeong A and curator Hans Ulrich Obrist for the campaign. All of which, once again, conveyed a sense of kudos for the house; a mix of cult and commercial heroes.

Of all the campaigns to steal the limelight, the most iconic has to be spring/summer 2024, starring Maggie Smith, who sits and stares right at you, armed with her Paseo bag. In another image she is sporting the Puzzle bag – an icon with an icon. Social media went wild, praising what was an unexpected choice (and compared it to the time Phoebe Philo at Céline cast the writer Joan Didion for a campaign).

OPPOSITE A Loewe campaign featured in a magazine circa 2015, showing its more 1980s slant.

OVERLEAF Loewe womenswear spring summer 2024: an artful setting.

LOEWE

OPPOSITE Jamie Dornan was part of the Loewe cohort at the 2024 Met Gala; he wore a Loewe look for the occasion.

RIGHT Aubrey Plaza wearing the much memed Loewe dress at the 75th Primetime Emmy Awards, January 2024.

Some of the images this time around, the brand said, were created through a process of photographing, printing, ripping out, superimposing and photographing again. The legendary actress was joined by Greta Lee and Dakota Fanning, actors Josh O'Connor and Mike Faist, model Fei Fei Sun, musician Taeyong, and artist Rachel Jones, all of whom carried different Loewe bags.

Meanwhile, the actor Jamie Dornan featured in the spring/summer 2024 menswear campaign and Aubrey Plaza would return – not only to give out the craft prize – but for the spelling bee-themed campaign *Decades of Confusion*, a tongue-in-cheek film on how to say the word "Loewe".

At the heart of all the campaigns – even those from the early days photographed by Steven Meisel and featuring Stella Tennant reading *Don Quixote* – is the idea of Loewe's multi-faceted identity. While fashion-driven, they are open to different ideas and inspirations, and have played a significant role in the rebrand of the Spanish house.

Other unexpected ways the brand has stopped us in our tracks is with such debuts as the Tomato Leaves candle, which caused ripples on TikTok. A whole article was dedicated to it in *Harper's Bazaar* where the editors just can't get their heads around how good it is – the smell, apparently, is spot on – spiralling into a wider discussion on Loewe candles, generally. As chic as you would imagine (some of the first ones took on the actual shape of a candle in its holder, which was perfectly surreal), they have become a lifestyle accessory in their own right. Of course, it's the accessories that cause a lot of the excitement at Loewe.

OPPOSITE The actress Alison Oliver at the Loewe womenswear autumn/winter 2024–25 show at Paris Fashion Week. She has featured in brand campaigns and worn looks on the red carpet.

ACCESSORIES

THE PUZZLE BAG IS BORN

Every big fashion house has a bag, or *the* bag. At Chanel, it's the 2.55; at Dior, it's the Saddle bag; at Fendi, it's the Baguette; and at Loewe, arguably it's the Puzzle bag. Instantly recognizable for its jigsaw-like construction and robust cuboid shape, it was the first new bag designed by Anderson, introduced in the spring/summer 2015 men's collection, shown in June 2014.

A top-handle version was shown at his womenswear show in September that year. And there have been countless versions since, making it one of the most coveted among the luxury arm candy world. Upon its release, the designer had told the press that he was looking at new ways to build a bag and had been questioning their structure.

Despite probably being the best-known Loewe bag, it is not the first Loewe bag. The Amazona style can take that title. It was first introduced in 1975, intended for a growing female workforce. The logic behind the design was that it was more design-led than a briefcase. It is a top-handle tote in technical bag terms, which is functional: it has a robust structure and

OPPOSITE Accessories galore backstage at the Loewe autumn/winter 2015–16 show.

features no decoration apart from a padlock. From time to time Stuart Vevers put the bag among his Loewe catwalk collection during his tenure at the house. Meanwhile Anderson flashed a tweedy version for autumn/winter 2016. For the maison's 175th anniversary, Anderson brought it back from the archives once more for the autumn/winter 2021 show, where he made it slightly smaller than the original and available in either square or rectangular shapes – the Amazona 19 Square and the Amazona 28, featuring removable and adjustable straps and a large-zipped compartment. The decision garnered plenty of press. The name Amazona is reported to be inspired by Greek myths of the Amazons, or warrior women. Available in vibrant Nappa calfskin, there's also the Amazona Anagram Jacquard version with interlocking Ls. And there have been more versions since, including a mini size. The brand describes it as being a house icon and a symbol of modernity, practicality and freedom. It does have a solid "proper" handbag feel to it, which can evolve once the straps are added.

Another house icon is the Flamenco style, which is thought to have debuted in the 1980s, relaunched by Vevers again in 2010. Anderson continues to include the bag, which takes its name from a Flamenco skirt, in Loewe collections with his own take. In 2015, he added knots instead of tassels on its sides where it pulls together. It is the perfect JW Anderson touch that just gives the bag a sense of subverted modernity. For spring/summer 2024, he introduced a new version of the Flamenco featuring a leather-woven doughnut chain strap, which gives it a rather decadent feel – colours include jewel tones – ideal for evening dressing or the autumn and winter months.

But, rather cleverly for a brand whose history lies in leather, Loewe has also managed to corner the summer market with its woven basket bags, a house signature, which lean into its

GHT All about
e accessories for
ring/summer 2016.

VERLEAF LEFT
scrunched up,
e Flamenco bag,
ewe autumn/
nter 2024–25.

VERLEAF RIGHT
loser look at the
cessories that have
ade the brand a hit
Loewe autumn/
nter 2020–21, here
ersion of
e Flamenco.

craftsmanship heritage. Woven in raffia, iraca palm, elephant grass and palm leaf by a global community of artisans, the bags are finished with leather straps and typically retail at a lower, more accessible, price point compared to the brand's other bags. They also come in a range of designs, shapes, styles and sizes, which have fast made them highly covetable, while ensuring the brand has traction all year round. The popular Font tote in raffia has a version that features a fluted edge, which makes it a distinctive design to add to a bag collection.

There are also examples among the Paula's Ibiza collection, a collaboration which began with Loewe in 2017. Paula's, a renowned Ibiza haunt in the 1970s, taken on by a German architect Armin Heinemann, became known for selling bohemian clothes and being something of a hippy lifestyle hub – Donna Summer, Jean Paul Gaultier and Freddie Mercury are among those who are said to have frequented it. By the end of 2000, it was no more. But in 2016, Loewe got in touch. Jonathan Anderson had visited Ibiza as a child and was familiar with the store. In 2017, a collaboration titled Loewe Paula's Ibiza debuted featuring womenswear and menswear, as well as accessories, with various bestselling ideas taken from the archive. It has become a recurring relationship every summer and combines the handicraft and art for which both names are known. Among the offering are raffia bags, which are made in Spain using raffia and iraca palm leaves that have been cultivated, harvested, sun-dried and hand-woven by artisans around the world, in Colombia, Morocco and Madagascar. Notably, for every bag sold, the house makes a donation to the local communities that hand-weave them. The idea is that the donation will help to provide university scholarships in Colombia; build a training school for craft in Madagascar; as well as provide humanitarian relief in the aftermath of

OPPOSITE The Gate bag, a street style favourite, spotted outside Vivienne Westwood during Paris Fashion Week, spring/summer 202

OVERLEAF Besides the Puzzle bag, the brand has made a name for itself for its raffia designs.

Morocco's 2023 earthquake. Silk scarf dresses, resin charms of oysters, bucket hats; colourfully woven versions of the Puzzle bag; elephant raffia beach bags, retro sunglasses and sandals boasting pebble hardware can also be found among the fun and characterful pieces. Again, it has been a clever way to combat the

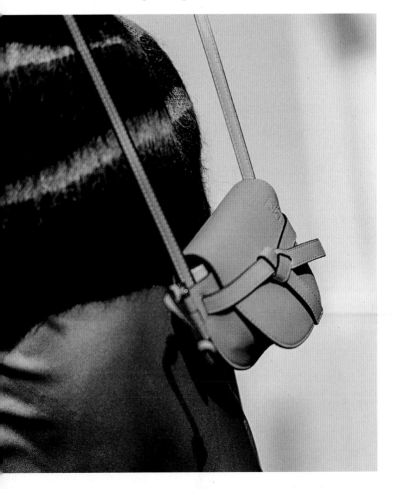

quandary of how to keep a leather brand relevant and desirable during summer.

In spring/summer 2018, the Gate bag came along. It is designed as a shoulder, crossbody, sling or belt bag and features a knotted leather detail across its front. It is another street style favourite, more playful and practical for everyday with its detachable and adjustable shoulder straps. Alessandra Ambrosio and Tilda Swinton have been spotted wearing it.

The Goya bag, which arrived for autumn/winter 2021, is a structured bag, very elegant, very neat and very desirable in line with the Hermès Constance owing to its chic strap. It fastens

with the Loewe anagram as the closure, and is in a flap style that feels classic; however, puffer versions (which make the fastening really stand out) in perfectly jarring Loewe colours cater to those wanting something a little more arty or quirky.

The Squeeze came along for autumn/winter 2023 and currently features versions bejewelled in beads to the look of a strawberry, passion fruit and kiwi fruit, which are really fun – and no doubt highly collectible. They are beautiful pieces of craftsmanship and come with a price tag to match. There are more simple and practical versions of the bag, though, in leather. The bag features a chain ruched through the top; and although it can be carried by the soft and puffy handle, it can also be worn on the shoulder.

One could argue it's in a similar vein to the Hammock bag, which is a signature shape for Loewe's women's shoulder bag range. It, too, can be worn multiple ways but is perhaps more overtly practical where the Squeeze is more dressy because of the chain detail.

For spring/summer 2023, there was the Paseo, a new addition to the house which was inspired by the Loewe archives. It is a similar shape, it is noted, to a bag from the Aire series with a flat, elliptical shape which is both striking and startling – there are versions that are more square in shape, akin to a satchel.

Just like the Flamenco bag, it features knots as part of the handle detailing, and comes in a variety of sizes. Taylor Russell, a Loewe house ambassador, featured in the spring/summer 2023 campaign wearing it – alongside the Anthurium plant top – elegantly posed as a ballet dancer. Culture and style publication *Highsnobiety* was already calling it an "It" piece in the making.

The Puzzle bag, of course, was an "It" bag even from the start. It is said to take over nine hours for the nine individual pieces of leather to be sewn together by the atelier. It is a recognizable

OPPOSITE
Focus on fabric and textures for spring/summer 2017.

OPPOSITE
...ing up the arm
...ndy and wrist
...ndy for spring/
...mmer 2022.

RIGHT
...e beaded dog bag,
...tumn/winter 2024.

favourite among the street style set as well as fashion editors. There are also variations on the original: the Mini Puzzle Fold tote, the Puzzle Fold tote, the Small Puzzle Edge, the Mini Puzzle Edge, the Small Puzzle and the men's Puzzle Fold tote... The Internet has dozens of column inches and Instagram snaps devoted to the Puzzle bag, which has offered options that were fun and playful – such spots – and luxe and practical. Kate Bosworth, Beyoncé, Naomi Campbell, Hari Nef and Jennifer Lawrence are among those who have been spotted wearing it over the years.

The Puzzle Fold tote debuted for autumn/winter 2023's pre-collection (the collections that get shown between the main autumn/winter and spring/summer seasonal shows), a riff on the original Puzzle and also, apparently, an archive Loewe design known as the Origami (sadly, it seems there are none to be found anywhere on resale sites). It is a tote which has been designed so that it can be easily folded down and, for example, packed into a suitcase or another bag for convenience and versatility when travelling.

It was after seeing the work of Knot On My Planet, which aims to stop the poaching of elephants and trafficking of ivory, that Anderson became interested in conservation, reported Vogue.com. He was introduced to the Samburu community of northern Kenya, which works closely with Save the Elephants. The Elephant Crisis Fund is a joint initiative between it and the Wildlife Conservation Network in partnership with the Leonardo DiCaprio Foundation, with the help of Knot On My Planet.

In 2018, in support of the Elephant Crisis Fund, Loewe partnered with Knot On My Planet to introduce a limited edition run of its tan Elephant bags, which are leather bags shaped like charming elephants, featuring the beadwork of the Samburu women. The bags retailed for £1,100, with 100 per

OPPOSITE A version of the Puzzle bag, Loewe, autumn/winter 2015–16.

RIGHT Loewe's elephant bag design, part of a roster of cute critter accessories, autumn/winter 2020–21 menswear.

OPPOSITE Model and influencer Kiwi Lee Han with a Loewe elephant bag outside the Loewe show, Paris Fashion Week, spring/summer 2023.

cent of that sum going toward conservation initiatives. Each bag featured unique decoration owing to the nature of the beadwork. Anderson's little leather critters – there has been a rabbit and panda as well as the elephant – were part of the Animals collection, and made the coin purse a mini "It" bag of its own. Indeed, the brand does mini coin purse versions of its other bags too, including the Goya and the Puzzle. These petite pieces have been joined over the years by further key charms and pins and bring an irreverent charm to the brand, making it playful and fun where other heritage brands might feel austere and unapproachable.

It has often been the accessories that have caused the brand to "go viral" – which is particularly true in the case of its shoes.

LEFT A sheep bag
design, menswear
autumn/winter
2020–21.

OPPOSITE Cat
accessories for
autumn/winter
2016–17.

VIRAL MOMENTS

ATTENTION-GRABBING DESIGNS

Fashion has had a predilection for an intriguing heel for some time: the late Karl Lagerfeld famously – and perhaps rather controversially – sent out a gun/pistol heel on a Chanel catwalk in 2008. While at Yves Saint Laurent, Stefano Pilati gave us the cage boot circa spring/summer 2009, and under its latest creative director Anthony Vaccarello we have had the YSL spelt out as the heel.

At Loewe, Anderson gave us a broken egg heel in 2021, for the spring/summer 2022 collection. Up top, it was about experimenting with proportions, but on the feet were heels on sandals of every surreal type. The broken egg, as though the heel had just pierced the shell; an upturned rose stem, so the petals squashed onto the floor at the heel tip; a nail polish heel; and a striped pink and white birthday candle heel. It was a gimmick that worked in his surreal hands to make the items collectible even if they weren't necessarily wearable (good luck finding a cobbler who could repair that heel tip!) Fashion Twitter, now X, notably weighed in.

OPPOSITE Ariana Grande, friend of the brand, wearing custom Loewe at The Met Gala 2024.

BELOW Attention to craft details got everyone talking about the menswear spring/summer 2025 collection, described by the brand as an act of restraint.

OPPOSITE Angelic wings for menswear autumn/winter 2023–24.

Fashion now is so much about moments going viral. It is no longer just the buyers and the press a fashion house seeks to impress, but the social media world at large. Which is not to say that is how Anderson approaches collections. But his ability to question and push, explore tension, try perceivably bonkers ideas in a luxury way is what makes his Loewe ideal for catching such moments. The designer himself has spoken about how social media has become quite bizarre and observed that the Internet only shows you what you want to see. The people, as it turns out, well – they want to see Loewe.

For the autumn/winter 2022 collection, there were more shoes to be excited about: the Loewe bow sandals spilled over the foot as though they had wrapped up a present, made even more poignant rendered in shiny silver. Above them, a bright pink dress boasted lips across the bust to make the whole look even more Elsa Schiaparelli in feel. They would show up on the red carpet.

It is also in this collection that balloons became a key theme, perched on busts as though the breast, or jammed into sandal straps. Shoes seemed also to be lost in contorted garments as what felt like a new twist on Schiaparelli's shoe hat. A statement

OVERLEAF On parade, the spring/summer 2022 finale

BELOW The balloon shoes, one of many shoe designs that has made the brand famous.

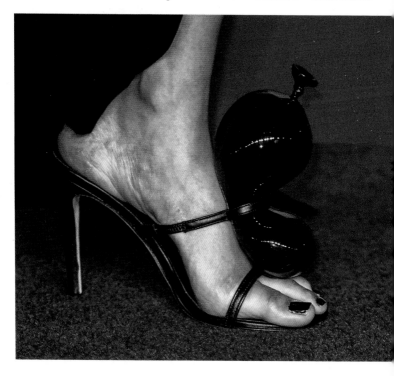

RIGHT Jake
Gyllenhaal and
Jeanne Cadieu attend
the 75th Anniversary
celebration screening
of *The Innocent*
during the 75th
Annual Cannes film
festival at the Palais
des Festivals, 2022.
He is wearing all
Loewe.

ABOVE The trouser boots, autumn/winter 2023–24.

neck feature on one look took the neck cushion into new fashio territory. There was a lot to look at in this collection.

Everyone, especially celebrities, became obsessed by a particular Loewe bomber jacket also in the autumn/winter 2022 collection Kendall Jenner and Hailey Bieber, as well as house ambassador Taylor Russell, were clocked wearing the puffer design – available in green or black – and which on the runway was worn with baggy trousers and those balloon sandals.

For autumn/winter 2023, Anderson continued the surreal streak with boots that looked like they were the tops of trousers complete with pockets and a fly-zipper detail. But, subtly done as they were, they didn't actually look as strange as they sound. Called the Toy Boot, the slouchy style further mimicked the ide of wearing baggy trousers in a smaller, micro-proportioned way. Emily Ratajkowski was spotted in the style.

RIGHT The Polly Pocket look for autumn/winter 23–24.

PPOSITE Plug/sink
les for menswear
tumn/winter
22–23.

GHT Floral
signs at Paris
shion Week,
ptember 2022.

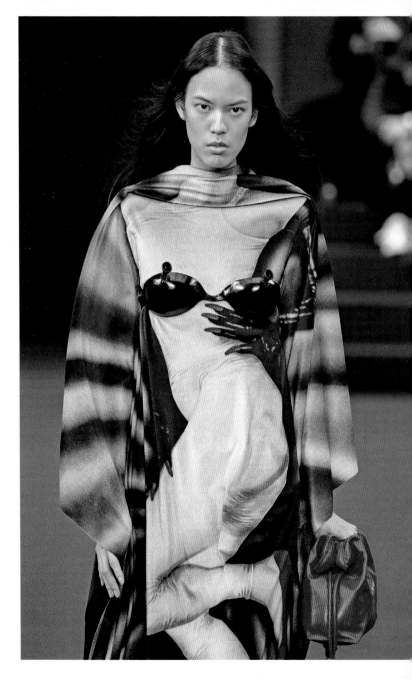

OPPOSITE Balloons
made for a surprise
style detail at Loewe
autumn/winter 2022.

RIGHT As worn by
Emma Corrin at The
Olivier Awards 2022.

LEFT A blank canvas backdrop for spring/ summer 2022.

The grass sneakers, or rather grass collection, appeared for menswear spring/summer 2023. During the actual presentation, the items that featured grass – which included sneakers, jeans, coats and trousers – featured real grass which had been created (grown?!) in partnership with the artist Paula Ulargui Escalona, who had cultivated chia plants and catswort ahead of the show. The effect was striking and quite magical. Notably, when the shoes became available in shops, the grass was not real – instead it was replicated using hand-embroidered raffia all over.

There were also coats covered in screens, which made for a technological contrast and a pointed note on how today everyone is consumed by the screen.

Technology fuelled even more Instagram feeds among the spring/summer 2023 womenswear collection, where Anderson made pixelated silhouettes that looked like the models were part of a computer game from the 1990s. The designer described it as like glitches. *Trompe l'oeil* taken to a new, meta level, it was a hoodie, trousers and T-shirt that got everyone talking.

Feet were festooned with shrivelled balloon shoes and this was the collection that also featured what *Bustle* called the "magic" dress that it reported had been freaking out Emma Watson's fans on Instagram. She had been pictured wearing the swathed, strapless design featuring jagged lines pointing up, and no obvious way to suggest how it was staying put – prompting a whole host of Harry Potter puns.

Off the catwalk, there have also been many moments – not small, but big – to keep Loewe fans talking.

In February 2023, Loewe was one of the fashion houses that dressed superstar Rihanna for her half-time performance at the Super Bowl – a cultural highlight of the year (Taylor Swift made the event even more popular in 2024, not because she

OPPOSITE Emma Watson's magical floating dress on th[e] catwalk.

played but because she attended it). All eyes are on that half-time show; for context, advertisers pay huge sums to advertise during transmission, such are the viewing figures.

A red catsuit formed the basis of the look, made from silk jersey with a matching cotton canvas flight suit and a made-to-measure corset sculpted in leather. Her appearance in the look was further heightened because it was her first live performance in five years, and she took the time to announce her second pregnancy. Later that year, Loewe introduced three pieces inspired by the Rihanna capsule look. A poppy-red aviator suit with zipped ankle cuffs; a version in black; and also black trousers.

From one superstar to another, Loewe dressed Beyoncé for her Renaissance tour. According to *Vogue.com*, her "hands-on" bodysuit was one of the most talked-about looks of the world

LEFT Rihanna performs during halftime at Super Bowl LVII, between Kansas City Chiefs and Philadelphia Eagles, wearing custom Loewe, February 2023.

OPPOSITE Grass designs for menswear, spring/ summer 2023.

RIGHT iPad designs also featured for spring/summer 2023 Loewe in complete contrast.

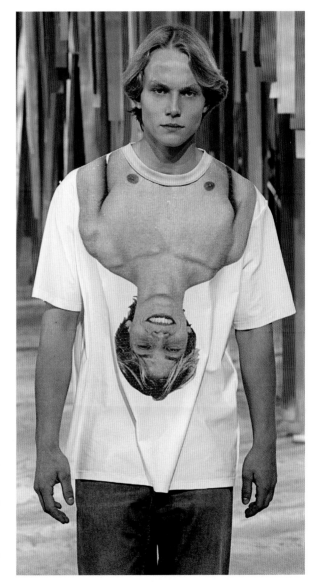

OPPOSITE "Arrgh!"
Menswear autumn/
winter 2022–23.

RIGHT Funny.
Menswear autumn/
winter 2022–23.

LEFT Making moves at Loewe spring/ summer 2022 womenswear.

OPPOSITE New proportions at Loewe spring/ summer 2023 womenswear.

tour – which featured many, many outfits by many, many fashion houses. Loewe made two looks for the star, both of which borrowed from the autumn/winter 2022 collection, which explored surrealist themes, sculptural forms and *trompe l'oeil* ideas. The bespoke pieces were created at the maison's ateliers in France and Spain by Loewe artisans, who worked in collaboration with the costume designer Shiona Turini. Loewe described the looks as blending futuristic ideas with a disco-era feel. The looks were high-shine meets robot and machine, and featured latex and 3D printed leather pieces. Surrealist hand

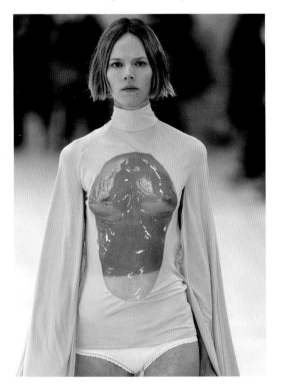

LEFT Freja Beha Erichsen models for spring/summer 202

OPPOSITE More balloons, autumn/ winter 2022–23.

OPPOSITE Toot toot,
beep beep. Loewe
autumn/winter
2022–23.

RIGHT A surrealist
mood for autumn/
winter 2022–23.

motifs featured on bodysuits (Beyoncé wore one as did her dancers), in chrome, silver, black, white and grey which was contrasted with red and gold.

From stage to screen, Anderson has been involved in the film *Challengers*, as its costume designer, with its stars wearing Loewe both in and out of the film. The film's director Luca Guadagnino (with whom Anderson worked on a spring/summer 2024 Loewe film) had been keen to work with Anderson ever since he saw his first collection. In an interview with *W Magazine*, Guadagnino explained how he thought Anderson would be great at doing the costumes because of his knowledge of the history of silhouette. Guadagnino had originally wanted to tap him for a TV series of *Brideshead Revisited* that never came to be. Anderson said that he liked the idea that people wouldn't necessarily know it was costume because the looks in the film are really everyday wear. The designer enjoyed obsessing over the details and thinking about what success and what brands looked like in America. Josh O'Connor, one of the film's stars, is a Loewe campaign stalwart.

It is the "I Told Ya" shirt worn by Zendaya and Josh O'Connor in the film – which retails for £225 – which has made many a headline. *L'Officiel* dubbed it the shirt of the summer in 2024. The story behind it, it said, is that in the mid-1990s a picture surfaced showing John F. Kennedy Jr. playing frisbee with his German Shepherd wearing a slogan T-shirt that read "I Told Ya". Because it resembled the one in the film, the Internet began to dissect these stories behind the T-shirt. It explained when JFK was inaugurated in 1961, his supporters wore pins with the slogan "I Told You So". Kennedy had won by a narrow margin against Richard Nixon. The slogan became popular again with JFK Junior's frisbee moment.

Loewe's contribution to *Challengers* doesn't stop there. For the press tour of the film, Zendaya has been wearing custom Loewe

RIGHT Zendaya in the now iconic "I Told Ya" Loewe T-shirt.

LEFT Zendaya at the March 2024 Australian premiere of *Challengers* in Sydney, Australia, in custom Loewe.

looks (as well as other designers) which speak to the tennis theme of the film. Her first outfit for the *Challengers* tour was a lithe, glistening green gown in sequins, featuring a person, tennis racket and tennis ball on it in black. Next, she wore a silver tennis dress with pleated skirt detailing – but it was the shoes that were the viral sensation: with tennis ball heels. An updated version, perhaps, of the egg, candle and rose.

Zendaya also wore Loewe at the after-party for the 2024 Met Gala, of which Loewe was the sponsor. The actress – who was also a Met Gala co-chair – wore a slate-grey gown at the event following the official opening of the Metropolitan Museum's latest fashion exhibition, Sleeping Beauties: Reawakening Fashion (which feels a little like what Anderson did at Loewe). The red carpet seemed to belong to two designers that night – John Galliano, of Maison Margiela, and Jonathan Anderson of Loewe, naturally. Loewe's friends and fashion family in

BELOW Zendaya in custom Loewe shoes for a *Challengers* photo call, 2024 in Rome, Italy.

OPPOSITE Up close
at the autumn/winter
2024–25 show.

RIGHT Greta Lee,
friend of the house
and campaign star,
at the Met Gala in
custom Loewe, 2024.

attendance included Dan Levy, Jonathan Bailey, Ambika Mod, Luca Guadagnino, Jamie Dornan, Mike Faist, Josh O'Connor, Ariana Grande and Greta Lee, who all wore custom looks. Brand ambassador Taylor Russell wore a 3D moulded bodice, a technique that had been developed for the spring/summer 2023 collection and racked up column inches in fashion publications. Alison Oliver, who is fronting the Paula's Ibiza campaign for spring/summer 2024, wore a trapeze coat which had been embroidered with crystals and a patchworked train. It had been made from antique garments and fabrics from the sixteenth century. Actress Ayo Edebiri wore a halterneck gown which had been crafted from hand-painted and hand-embroidered guipure lace. It gave the illusion of 3D flowers. All this created a magical evening for the house, compounding its success, relevance and influence under Anderson.

In an interview with *The Daily Telegraph* in early 2024, Anderson noted that he didn't believe in being a 70-year-old designer and pointed out that young people needed to take over. He felt working 10 years above and 10 years below was the sweet spot. He was aware his role had a shelf-life. He has now been at Loewe over 10 years. And, right now, still seems well placed on his shelf: it seems he can do no wrong – his spectacular spring/summer 2025 menswear show in Paris was a case in point. A front row full of the most exciting names in film and a runway showcasing some of the most exciting and beautiful craft-laden ideas in fashion. How long Anderson will be at Loewe is probably up to him, but he's certain to leave a lasting legacy.

Loewe is arguably among the longest-standing heritage houses, having weathered the test of trends and time to boast a history even longer – and still going – than some of the best-known names in fashion.

OPPOSITE Brand ambassador Taylor Russell flying the Loewe flag at The Met Gala, 2024.

LEFT Loewe creative
director Jonathan
Anderson takes a
bow at the autumn/
winter 2020–21 show.

INDEX

CREDITS

The publishers would like to thank the following sources for their kind permission to reproduce the pictures in this book.